mourning m

In a world that marginalizes, castigates, and abuses Black women, Ree Botts loves us. She loves us as she exposes the raw truth of those external pressures on our bodies, minds, and spirits. She loves us defiantly and brilliantly, treats us with care and attention, as she crafts a poetics infused praxis of resilience and regeneration. In this book, she fearlessly reveals her personal harm and invites us to develop an empathetic depth needed for collective change. Hers is a praxis of self-healing and freedom, and she generously holds out a hand to guide us all, too. Healing is messy and the practice of healing is hard; still, she pulls us along, persistently. She breaks through tangles and reveals the spikes that threaten within narrative, deftly composed poetic form, and an interweaving of spell-inducing metaphor. Particularly in the integration of poems written in her teenage years, Ree shows us a clarity in her wisdom and healing. She loves us Black women and that is the greatest testament to her daring in this important work, for love is the foundation of any movement that truly shapes the world and the people within it anew.

RAINA J. LEÓN, PHD
author of *Profeta Without Refuge*

mourning my inner[blackgirl]child

reelaviolette botts-ward
brittany botts
ree botts
& all the selves in between

NOMADIC PRESS

OAKLAND

111 FAIRMOUNT AVENUE
OAKLAND, CA 94611

BROOKLYN

475 KENT AVENUE #302
BROOKLYN, NY 11249

WWW.NOMADICPRESS.ORG

MASTHEAD

FOUNDING AND MANAGING EDITOR
J. K. FOWLER

ASSOCIATE EDITOR
MICHAELA MULLIN

EDITOR
RAINA J. LEÓN

MISSION STATEMENT

Nomadic Press is a 501 (C)(3) not-for-profit organization that supports the works of emerging and established writers and artists. Through publications (including translations) and performances, Nomadic Press aims to build community among artists and across disciplines.

SUBMISSIONS

Nomadic Press wholeheartedly accepts unsolicited book manuscripts. To submit your work, please visit www.nomadicpress.org/submissions

DISTRIBUTION

Orders by trade bookstores and wholesalers:

Nomadic Press Distribution
orders@nomadicpress.org
(510) 500-5162

Small Press Distribution,
spd@spdbooks.org
(510) 524-1668 / (800) 869-7553

mourning my inner[blackgirl]child

This book was made possible by a loving community of chosen family and friends, old and new.

For author questions or to book a reading at your bookstore, university/school, or alternative establishment, please send an email to info@nomadicpress.org.

Cover artwork and author portrait by Arthur Johnstone

Published by Nomadic Press, 111 Fairmount Avenue, Oakland, CA 94611

Second printing, 2021

LIBRARY OF CONGRESS CATALOGING-IN-PUBLICATION DATA

reelaviolette botts-ward 1993 –
Title: *mourning my inner[blackgirl]child*
P. CM.
Summary: *mourning my inner[blackgirl]child* is an unabashed exposure of girlhood fragility, ancestral grieving, and embodied remembering. In her excavation of multiple pasts and multiple selves, botts-ward journeys through intimate encounters with her mother(s), her home, her body, and her precarity. As she mourns her deepest wounds, botts-ward lays bare the im/possibilities of Black girlhood, slippages of Black motherhood, and matrilineal legacies of abuse. In telling her story, she tells so many of our own. botts-ward's poetry invites Black women deeper into our healing and centers the little girl within herself who has a sacred word for the world.

[1. POETRY. 2. BLACK GIRLHOOD. 3. BLACK MOTHERHOOD. 4. ABUSE. 5. HEALING. 6. AMERICAN GENERAL.]
I. III. TITLE.

LIBRARY OF CONGRESS CONTROL NUMBER: 2021932303

ISBN: 978-1-7363963-5-3

mourning my inner[blackgirl]child

reelaviolette botts-ward
brittany botts
ree botts
& all the selves in between

**NOMADIC
PRESS**

for brax,

baby child
brave soul

still healing
in heaven

for britt britt,

the baby child
of a baby child

.

healing

hurts harder
than hurting

but it's worth it
she deserves it

A RITUAL FOR READING

one

visit blackwomxnhealing.com/book[1]
 to guide you through this experience

read alongside
sight and sound
read alongside
breath

.

two

each poem ends
with a footnoted citation[2]
of a black womxn artist
whose work
inspired my words
watch her film
hear her song
read her poetry.

---

[1] While this work can be richly experienced solely in analog form, it is written to be read alongside blackwomnhealing.com/book. blackwomxnhealing.com houses creative communal care work curated for Black womxn, by Black womxn. As a multimedia artist, this virtual component allows for a multimodal experience of my poetry that provides texture and nuance to the work. Use this site as a guide through this book. As you experience each poem, I invite you to experience its corresponding song/ image/ film. I invite you to journey with me in multiple dimensions.

[2] Inspired by Christen Smith's #citeblackwomen, I name the black womxn scholars and artists who deeply inform my poetry. Details about their work can be found at blackwomnhealing.com/book.

three

do not
read this
all at once

slow down
take breaks
take baths
burn sage
light candles
drink water
journal
about what
comes up

breathe deep
breathe often
this shit is
heavy..

CONTENTS

CLASSROOM GUIDE

INTRODUCTION

when i was a girl
i had a woman inside me
when i became a woman
i had a girl inside me
i never wanted to be a woman
when i was a girl
i never wanted to be a girl
when i was a woman

/

i had to murder the child in me.. it was the only way i would be well.. as a woman of twenty three years who yearned to be grown up.. i convinced myself *the only way to win womanhood is to make girlhood die*.. with deep shame.. about all the ways i had carried her wounds within me.. i made the choice to choke her dead.. for all the ways she forced me outside myself.. for all the ways she shielded me from growth.. with deep shame.. about how immature i had been.. how unwise.. naive.. gullible.. how vulnerable to this world and it was all her fault because she would not let me be woman..

/

i never
wanted
to be a
woman
when i
was a
girl
i never
wanted

to be a
girl
when i
was a
woman

/

who was to blame for this fragmentation.. this impossibility of a self.. these wounds.. the way they cut into my flesh with no warning.. without my consent.. who is to blame for these blistered scars that do not scrub up off my arms and glow in the dark when i ain't sleeping.. who forced the hands of this suicide.. who is the cause of this death..?

...

at twenty-seven years old, i will blame whiteness and its perceived supremacy. i will blame capitalism and its robbing of space.. time.. intimacy.. the scarcity it produces. the ways it seeps into black family and dictates who a mother can or cannot be to her children because of precarity. i will blame patriarchy and its promise to protect me. all the ways it lied to me. its refusal to protect girls like me. its failure to protect any girls at all. its inherent impossibility. the way it blends/ bends/ breaks/ merges into rigidity at the interlocking of intersectional.. ancestral.. generational.. gendered.. racialized wounds. the way it secretes its demand for submission into the bloodline of every woman to wear Sibert.Botts. LaViolette behind her name.

i will not blame my mother.. whose mother was the daughter of a woman raised by the formerly enslaved.. i will not blame inner blackgirls for battering and bruising in attempts to salve and soothe.. i will not blame women who were black and bruised for fumbling through the wilds of the west with no map.. no mask.. no compass.. for inheriting illusive love languages birthed from the afterlife of slavery[1]..

.

in this season, i am learning to find balance between blame.. grace.. accountability.. to name my pain and be unashamed of the scars that made me human.. to claim my rage and point with precision to the source.. the seed.. the root.. to hold humans accountable for hurting me.. to hold me accountable for hurting me.. to ground my healing in grace..

i am learning to love britt britt in all the ways she deserved to be loved back then.. to become the mother to myself that my mother never could be to me back then.. because this world forced laviolette into silence.. sleep.. submission.. depression.. invisibility.. i am learning that no woman of my bloodline is to blame for the harm her inner[blackgirl]child endured.. i am learning how heavy it feels tryna be the one to mend matrilineal wounds..

i am learning to mourn my inner[blackgirl]child.. to grieve the innocence she lost.. to account for the suffering she normalized as blackgirlhood.. i am learning how to allow myself to shed shrieking tears for her.. to honor her for doing her very best to curate a life she felt was safe for me..

i am learning that this healing is work.. that i will feel weary.. weighed down.. stuck.. in flux throughout this process of excavation.. i am learning to take breaks.. to lean in and out of the weight at the rhythm my body requests of me.. to be in my joy sometimes.. to allow myself the pleasures of comfort.. care.. warmth in my womb.. hope.. peace.. levity.. i am learning to "[find] god in myself and.. [to] love her fiercely..[2]"

.

---

[1] Hartman, Saidiya. Lose your mother : a Journey Along the Atlantic Slave Route. New York : Farrar, Straus and Giroux, 2007.

[2] Shange, Ntozake. *For Colored Girls Who Have Considered Suicide / When the Rainbow Is Enuf.* Scribner Poetry. 1975.

~~the only way~~
~~to win~~
~~womanhood~~
~~is to make~~
~~girlhood die~~
the only way
to win
womanhood
is to

LET
GIRLHOOD
LIVE

i made
amends
for that
death
brought
britt britt
back to life
she is the
true author
of this story

inner child healing
for black women
with black girls
inside them[3]

---

[3] Inner[blackgirl]child healing is a Black woman's journey of reclaiming the Blackgirlhood
she never fully had access to due to the intersections of sexism, racism, and the
adultification that challenged the freedoms of her youth.

my healing journey has been deeply transformed by Adult Children of Alcoholics and Dysfunctional Families' (ACA) 12 Steps of Recovery[4]. through ACA, i learned the power of inner child healing and initiated a reckoning with the generational patterns of dysfunction that led to my childhood suffering. yet, while ACA has been a true gift in my recovery, it has failed to account for the structural, systemic and institutional violences which shaped the legacies of dysfunction within my family.

.

my inner child is a black mother's child.. her mother's inner child is a black mother's child.. being the black daughter of a black mother in a nation rooted in hatred for your people is the foundation of the dysfunction within our families.

blackgirl childhoods been under attack since the birth of the first baby girl in the hold of the middle passage.. blackgirl childhoods been under attack since master's desire for premature wombs to produce the next generation of chattel slavery.. this trauma, the im/possibility of blackgirlhood passed down by each generation of our mothers, is the context in which we come to know our generational wounds.

i will not
blame
our inner
blackgirls
who been
battered
and bruised

---

[4] Adult Children of Alcoholics and Dysfunctional Families is a 12 Step program that provides literature and fellowship for adults seeking healing from dysfunctional childhoods. While neither of my parents were alcoholics, ACA has given me language to make sense of the ways that their parents' alcoholism and dysfunction influenced how they raised me. ACA introduced me to transformative inner child healing and continues to support my journey to self recovery.

for battering
and bruising
in attempts to
salve and soothe

.

inner[**blackgirl**]child, one word[5], affirms that the inner blackgirl in each of us black women had a right to her childhood.. she rescued herself the best way she knew how from gendered.. racialized.. sexualized violence.. she survived abuse that was generational.. perpetual.. pervasive.. she was just a child.. carrying the burdens of a woman.. a child deserving of her youth..

that child in each of us still suffers in the aftermath of her abuse.. that child inside our mothers is still struggling too.. we become women who work at love the best way we know how.. no one ever taught us how to do this.. no one ever taught us how to soothe this..

ancestral grieving gives us language to grapple with the im/possibilities of our grandmothers' girlhoods.. to name what gets passed down.. to face what was lost.. to acknowledge the im/possibilities of black motherhoods.. to reckon with lingerings of matrilineal suffering..

alchemy and remedy get passed down, too.. from a grandmother to the youngest blackgirl child.. from her astral realm to my altar.. fragmented tales of suffered survival.. anecdotes of ancestral memory.. i conjure hope

---

[5] In "On Being at Home with Myself: Blackgirl Autoethnography as Research Praxis," Robin M. Boylornw coins Blackgirl as one word to "make [the words] touch on paper the way they touch in [our] everyday existence."(49) The title of my book, and much of my Blackgirl musings, are inspired by her unapologetic centering of the duality of the twoness of our identities that are always experienced all at once.

Boylorn, Robin. On Being at Home With Myself: Blackgirl Autoethnography as Research Praxis. *International Review of Qualitative Research*, Vol. 9 No. 1, Spring 2016; (pp. 44-58) DOI: 10.1525/irqr.2016.9.1.44

from the mothers who are no longer here.. who bring peace in my process of healing..

.

my little
girl self
sensed
ties to
spirit
world
through
women
on the
other
side

my inner[blackgirl]child be indigo spirit.. blue soul child.. sun moon child.. she, like every blackgirl she know, birthed from an intimacy with astral planes.. returned to this earth from cosmos.. inherited sacral wisdom as birthright.. knows, in the depth of her being, how to be whole and well.. knows, in her body's intelligence, how to restore and release.. i am a woman.. learning to listen.. learning to let her lead..

let me
guide you
home
to your
soul

let me
take you
back

to your
spirit

trust me
i know
the way

/

it is my hope that every black woman who reads this will be invited into herself.. to tend to the wounds of her girlhood and reclaim the inner[blackgirl]child within.. with deep love, with deep care, with deep gratitude.. i welcome you into my dark parts..

THIS BOOK IS WRITTEN FOR ADULT AUDIENCES

Though this collection of poems centers Blackgirlhood, it is not written to be read by Blackgirls. This work is heavy, intense, explicit, candid, unfiltered, and vivid. It is written from an adult's perspective about sexual abuse and violence to support adult Black women in their processes of inner child healing. Thus, it is not appropriate for youth viewing.

BLACKGIRL BLUESOUL

in one moment in time, on one day in june, in my twenty third year of life, the ground slipped from under my feet and suddenly i was uprooted.. i heard a word from a girl i once knew and it shifted the meaning of my lifetime.. unprotected she said.. *unprotected all your life..*

it had been ten years since i commenced the mourning of my black girlhood.. a thirteen year old grieving the loss of her self..

i chucked my converse chuck taylors across the schuylkill river and traded them in for some too tight tango heels.. held my own virginity in my hand for the first time.. finally felt i knew what my vagina was made for.. fornicated with devils and sung old school blues.. bound myself to belonging.. battled depression in daisy dukes. thigh high boots. crop tops. knee high socks. satin lingerie.. longed for the gaping hole in my chest to be filled - even when i did not know it existed.. existed in the world so naked and bare that i was never made aware of it..

there i was on her living room sofa, sippin' sparkling cider like it wasn't soda.. serenaded by the way she placed synonyms and verbs together to vividly paint a picture of those ten years between thirteen and twenty three.. she told me my childhood had happened all wrong, my mother had birthed me and raised me all wrong. protection was never possible for girls like me. security was not deserved for girls like me.. and i realized how vulnerable i had been to the entirety of the world for the entirety of my life..

how easy it was for someone in some small moment to tell me all the things no one had ever loved me enough to say.. rose colored glasses fell from crystalized eyes and crashed into concrete like champagne glasses fallen from her kitchen counter in slow motion.. i could not counter her argument.. only could nod and dance a dangerous two step with my heart.. carrying burdens i never buried deep enough..

burned my hands in the batter but it still tasted sweet.. drank the juice of my killer's cum and it still tasted sweet.. never told all sweet things were not meant for consumption.. until now. the day life engulfed me and forced me to sink inside myself.. i saw myself for the first time through the lens of a world that never loved me.. i remain terrified of that site..

stayed up in connecticut cold 'til thirteen o'clock in the morning shedding never ending tears for my precarity.. felt the little lost girl tugging on my heart.. saw who she always needed me to be, who i could never become for her..

i had to do something different.. had to say something more real.. owed it to myself to become a voice of rigorous truth.. brutal and burdening honesty.. to go to that dark purple place in my memory when i stood on the side of the road, when i was abandoned. stranded. unclothed. unknown. unprotected. neglected. disrespected. distraught.. i had to go to that place on the side of that road, and dig..

this is the digging up of my truth.. the transition from my thirteen year old memory to my twenty third reality.. and the years that still linger in their wake.. i turn to these pages to cover me.. and i cover these pages to heal..[1]

---

[1] "Whether high, whether low, I'm often feeling like I gotta go, get away, escape the pain, I guess all I'm really tryna say is I don't wanna be alone."
Alone. Brittany Tanner + SOL Development. SOL of Black Folks. 2018.

INNER[BLACKGIRL]CHILD

they say
inner child[2]
will return me
to my / self
they say
inner child
will save
my life

but my
inner child
be blackgirl
she ain't never
knew much
about living

she can't barely
recall a time
when she wasn't
already grown

how chasing
a traumatized
child in me
gon save
my life?

---

[2] In Adult Children of Alcoholics Dysfunctional Families, there has been no way to make sense of my upbringing as an Adult [BlackGirl] Child of a dysfunctional family. I needed to write this book to name myself as a grown girl healing from a racialized gendered experience that needs explicit recognition in my healing process.

there is a
blackgirl
within
every
blackwomxnhealing[3]
she be gateway to spiritual selves
healer of intergenerational wounds
divine relation to mother ancestors
she birth
intergenerational healing

for every woman
of our bloodline
who couldn't[4]

---

[3] blackwomxnhealing.com frames "inner[blackgirl]child work as a tool to critically examine the ways intergenerational and ancestral trauma has informed one's own life, a way to study the patterns of passed down pain, grief, abuse, and internalized oppression, a way to name why your mother raised you the way her mother raised her.."

[4] "Black girls are likened more to adults than to children and are treated as if they are willfully engaging in behaviors typically expected of Black women.. [This has] stripped Black girls of their childhood freedoms.. and makes Black girlhood interchangeable with Black womanhood."
Morris, Monique. *Pushout.* The New Press. 2016.

CAREFREE BLACKGIRL

i was raised
in ribboned
rainbows

wrote
carefree blackgirl
codebook
in preteen diaries
before there was ever
a hashtag

*ree*centered reality
by mrs. moon
*ree*configured earth
in cornered bedroom closet
ran miles away from world
in lily pasted living room
rode bicycle boats
'cross cluttered kitchen cabinets
danced disco diva
on dusty dining room tables

rained on my own parade
in bubbled bathtub
to teach six year old self
even rainbows
know their share of showers

found my soul as child of
chalkboard scratchings

curated
imaginary space
for girls like me
to be free

and i was
free

every time
i crafted
cardboard boxes
into
makeshift high-heels
with my superhuman
synchronated sister

every time
crayola
cracked open
mystery colors
in my palm

every time
i drew
brown girl
on
white page
attached
ballies and bows
to lopsided head
braided
silky satin extensions
and afro puffs
drew in swoop bangs
and beaded bangles
named her

Khareeyiesha Fhaleiyesha LaViolette

created images
of myself
for myself
when
no one else
in the world
would

. . .

i made magic
in the home
you made for me
mama

grew up knowing
world different
because of you
mama

brought up
seeing rainbows
in everything
mama

because
you were the
sunshine
in everything
mama

thought
the world would

love me
like you loved me
mama

love me lingering
and love me good

never knew
the world
ain't feel like home
til the day
the showers came
the parade stopped
and there was no more room
for crayola markings[5]

[5] "The children.. they become the living people of the house, the house lives in them."
Broom, Sarah. *The Yellow House.* Grove Press. 2019.

WHAT WE CALL YOU

mother,

never knew your name was LaViolette
until age ten
all we ever knew you as was mama

mama,

never knew your name was loneliness
until age eleven
all we ever knew you as was sunshine

sunshine,

never knew your name was depression
until age twelve

all we ever knew you as was home

home,

never knew
          you never existed

until age thirteen.[6]

---

[6] "If I could, I'd give you the world. Wrap it all around you."
Angel. Anita Baker. The Songstress. 1983.

DITCH

dug
        deeper than i ever did.

didn't think

              diggin'

felt like this.

like muck under guck
of dingy bathroom tubs
that mama never made us scrub down

like loose limbs. like landlords at yo' porch
filthy laundry in yo' pantry. fruit trees in yo' dirt
uncatered to. peaches and pineapples
been sittin' on this counter for thirteen months

walls stained. teeth stained. heart stained.

house never in order.
        home never in order.
               heart never in order

        ....

the same tree that birthed me
hung me like strange fruit
then watched my open wounds rot
buried me right next to myself
nobody cared enough to stitch me up
i handed them their shovels

11

let them dig me up

> never knew the ditch they dug out
> my soul. one by one. in a row
> they took turns diggin' at me

like them peaches and pineapples
on that counter been sittin' there
for thirteen months. for thirteen years
i wondered

where my self went
between whose fingertips did i

> *slip?*

what warm bosom nurtured me?
from whose nectar did i suck
the ripest raw?

no one
i tasted nothing
like roots or soil grounding.

who ever warned me
to love self more than i love this world
'cause world won't

> /catch me when i fall
> when the sweet taste of georgia peach
> blossoms and bursts in one bite
> when i pick my first sour honey suckle
> and realize this life ain't sweet[7]

---

[7] "Blood on the leaves and blood at the root."
Strange Fruit. Cassandra Wilson. New Moon Daughter.1995.

THE ONLY FREEDOM IS DYING, GIRL

she haunts me
the demon
of my youth
the child
who is dying

purple pink
stockings
lavender lace
church socks
innocently
horrifying
holding my bare heart
in her hand

sings to me
sweet lullabies
of a fairy tale
i almost knew
reassuring me
there is no hidden truth

> *memories scar your mind*
> *make mirrors mimic*
> *matronly mourning*
> *in the morning you remember.*
> *whose mastery mattered more*
> *mama's and the maid's*
> *or murdering men*
> *who always got away?*

i see her silhouette
in the moonlit gaze
lost
used
a monotonous haze
she invites me to play
swings and seesaw
i saw her at the swings
by the seesaw
soon as i came to play
she ran away

she sits by the nectar tree
taunting me
waiting for me
to set her free
from this insane world
where

> *everyone has lied to you, girl*
> *everyone has let them dig you, girl*
> *everyone knows the only freedom*
> *is dying, girl*

she unearths me
reveals me to the moon
leaves me dangling
in her bare shadow

naked
as i was
on preteen lover's couch
as he etched his cum
into my skin
i let him dig me up
and dig me up

naked

as i was
in favorite uncle's bed
as he carved out
his piece of me
they let him dig me up
and dig me up
naked

as i was
on this page
as i am
forced to face
this narrow grave
the absence of her
and the presence of her
still

she stands still
in my shadow
i stare at her
and wonder
if anyone
ever heard her
alone at night
shedding tears that
burst out from her gut

gutted out the ditch
empty
nothing left but a
fractured bluesoul
attempting to stitch itself
but she's no doctor

memories scar your mind
make mirrors mimic
matronly mourning
in the morning you remember
whose reaction mattered more
mama's and the maid's
or the murdering men
who always got away

she leaves me
drowning
in my own blood
witnessing
the pre-crucifixion
of the girl

who is not ready to die
who is too afraid to die
who tugs on my sleeve
who cannot leave me alone

i remind her,

> *everyone has lied to you, girl*
> *everyone has let them dig you, girl*
> *everyone knows the only freedom*
> *is dying, girl*[8]

---

[8] "See, this is what that voice in your head says when you try to get peace of mind.. I gotta find peace of mind, I gotta find peace of mind."
I Gotta Find Peace of Mind - Live. Lauryn Hill. MTV Unplugged No. 2.0. 2002.

THE BLOOD IS ON HER HANDS

blood stains
taint her
thousand dollar white dress

make her feel as
tethered and tarnished
as tailored train
trailing in the dress' shadow

> *sink into the dress.*
> *sink into the ditch.*

> *wash your hands of the waves.*
> *wake for wars. stay unstitched*

how heavy a burden it is
to wear those layers of lies
on her skin

skin sticks to tulle
like tampered tulips
on tile floors
forgetting
forbidden fruit
is only a false remedy

remembering
who lived before the death
revisiting what was left
a beautiful mystery
inside her

bloody hands
haunted by the halos
of girlhood
who hid demons beneath
thousand dollar white dresses

uncomfortable
unable to find language
to let them know
how lust and love left
loss of life inside her
left her lonely
longing for those
lullabies
little girls sang,

> *hang head low*
> *hit left foot*
> *to the ground*
> *right foot*
> *to the ground*
> *take off running*
> *somewhere*
> *off the road*
> *somewhere far*
> *alone*

dragging demons
under dresses
that have no place
here anymore

> *sink into the dress.*
> *sink into the ditch.*

wash your hands of the waves.
wake to wars. stay unstitched

no one knows
who is hidden
beneath those layers
of fancy fabric
fucking fluff and faille
and forced facades

who is suffocating
in silky styrofoam boxes
and bent barbie doll
silicone
synthetic
ceramic design like
Build - a - Girl
like
too many hands
had a hand
in her making

surrounded
yet always alone
engulfed
yet isolated

they love
what they think
they know

the little girl
who ripped heads off
all her barbie dolls
the young woman
who let them stamp her self

Exhibit A
assembly lined
her womanhood

they labeled little ladies
princess
primped and pressed them
painted pretty polish
on picture perfect plastic
pathetic
preparing ballroom parties
pretending to be happy
inside they all are dying

inside her dress
she's trying
to keep death
from her mascara lining
to conceal the demons
within the lining
of her
thousand dollar white dress
feeling an eruption
beneath her
thousand dollar white dress

blood
boiling in her bones
blood
dripping at her feet
she is not the girl
they imagined she should be

but she reminds herself
        hiding is all we've ever known.

she is their royalty
and her own worst nightmare
the proof lie in the blood
and the blood is on her hands

> *hang head low*
> *hit left foot*
> *to the ground*
> *right foot*
> *to the ground*
> *take off running*
> *somewhere*
> *off the road*
> *somewhere far*
> *alone*

cries of the lifeless
still haunt her

so she sinks
        into the dress
and she sinks
        into the ditch

she washes her hands
of the waves
she awakens to wars
she remains unstitched[9]

---

[9] "Sink into the dress, sink into the ditch."
Tainted Illusions. Ree Botts. 2016.

STRANDED

knew no one was coming
for pick up
after school. pleats in
school uniform skirt wrinkled from
sleeping on classroom floors
past midnight
alone
knew no one was coming
for pick up

from ball. crown tilted
on top of crinkled curls
cream heels dangling
between two fingers
of left hand
on the side of that road
crossed on float during
homecoming parade
nostalgically recalls
the wave. the sash.
the children
waving with adoration
a sea of smitten faces

> *who do they think i am?*

i am the girl on the side of the road.

it is midnight
i stand barefoot
on that same concrete

chiffon wrinkles
line
thousand dollar white dress
tulle piled on tulle
too much tulle to walk away
comfortably
like Cinderella
after the lights went down
the glass slipper
came off
and i realize
i belong with the ashes
i belong to no one

here i am all over again

i nostalgically recall

the high school janitor
vacuuming 'cross classroom floors
where i lay my head to rest
past midnight
balled up letterman sweater
for makeshift pillow
rub my legs together
to keep warm
i was not homeless

but no one was home
no one was coming
to pick me up
from the side of Church road
no car was driving by to save me
no car had no place to even take me

i was always the girl
on that side of the road
alone
the side where no one would ever come[10]

---

[10] "Lonely, lonely, how I be. Lonely, lonely, cuts so deep."
Lonely. Jamila Woods. Heaven. 2016.

PERFORMING MY WHOLE FUCKIN LIFE

i
a fragile
fragmented
blackgirlwoman[11]
have been
performing
my whole fuckin life
like my fuckin life
depended on it

.

frail bones
of baby child
born too soon
and too late
in a spacetime
unfamiliar

.

five years old
body of christ
christian stage
god's little girl
spittin'
im gonna save the world
feelin' so compelled

---

[11] Shange, Savannah. Black Girl Ordinary: Flesh, Carcerality and the Refusal of Ethnography. *Transforming Anthropology Vol 27*.

in that charge

.

thirteen years old
sharing details of a rape
that took place
on body of christ
christian stage

thirteen years old
sharing details of a rape
as if it were unfamiliar

thirteen years old
sharing details of a rape
on stage
that never happened to me
it didn't happen to me

.

never knew
how to hold
that pain

still don't.

.

twenty three years old
a sash. a wave
homecoming parade
stuck on stage
in feminine silence

screaming in the wake
of my feminine silence

> *let me out of this*
> *heavy dress*
> *burdened garb*

> *let me be free*
> *let me be ree*

i did not create this
you molded me
into your liking
forced my curves
to fill out
the outlined form
of your yearning

.

twenty three years old
i try to break free
from performance

but that abused
little girl
of god
whose story
i vowed to tell
she is still a
performance
i am still a
performance

.

twenty seven years old
i'm yearning for truth
forreal
to put pieces of myself
back together
on my own terms

twist and turn at night
tryna not be an avatar
but i wake
and wash face
and pretend
i am a character
in a fiction
each day

.

i am
the nice girl
the sweet girl
the soft girl
the pretty girl
the prissy girl
the
never
quite
knew
how
to
be
proper girl

the multiple selves girl
the southern belle girl

the philly bird girl
the round the way girl
the ghetto girl
who never even lived
in the ghetto girl
the never could fit
neat into barbie girl
the always boxed into
barbie girl
the too deep
the too shallow

.

the budding
the blossoming

the baby child
that never finished
growing up

the premature
baby girl
turned
grown woman
too soon

.

i am
the moons
of the past
the passion
of the present
the prism
of the future

but that is fiction
because
i am fuckin
broken
scarred
scared
bruised
abused

i been performing
we been performing
our whole fuckin life

.

left back stage
with a sash
and a wave
smeared lipstick
bobby pinned
tilted crown
heavy gown
stuck

singing
to herself   .
offkey
longing
for that set
to never end
but it always ends
and she has no friends

just a mirror of
shattered selves

who never
keep her warm
who wander
beyond their borders
who break her windows
then walk away
come back
      in nightmares
            haunt her
            taunt her

she
is always referred to as me
the light brown blackgirl
who dared to dream

.

maybe
all blackgirls like me
could ever be is
performers

practice
perfectly paved road
of being real
of never fully
feeling
the realness
of the rawest
parts of our
vulnerability
because
could we ever
really afford
to *feel* this?

could i ever
really afford to
not be that girl?

.

maybe
blackgirls like me
all batshit crazy

but maybe
we just trying
our best
to get free[12]

12 "Stop looking for your reflection to wave back at you. You are the same person."
Instructions on Being. Tank and the Bangas. Think Tank. 2013.

EMBODIED BRUISING

girls grow up trained to perfect pretty.. if people call you beautiful that's all you'll ever need to be.. if you don't believe you're beautiful you have nothing more to live for.. and everyone say the little light girls are the pretty girls.. and everyone say the slim thick girls are the pretty girls..

no one say that pretty is made up and these fucked up social constructs constrain imaginaries of who blackgirls must be.. and when you are the blackgirl that blackgirls must be you see yourself as (no)body.. as (a) body.. as perception/ deception/ missrepresentation.. never fittin' in high yella skinned stereotyped tragic mulatta.. wishin' you was born brown so they don't question your intentions.. so your people could see you as whole and know shallow beauty hurt (every)body that is black, even the ones privileged and praised.. //

my relationship with body always been complicated by pale brown skin.. by girlhood.. by sexual assault.. by imagining this temple made for the world and never for me.. soul housed in shape that signals rape and rituals of wronging.. invites the uninvited.. makes brown and pale men entitled to my insides..

> *my birth into blackness*
> *made my gendered body*
> *unprotectable..*

since age thirteen my curves caved in and made men imagine they should have their way with me.. as a child i felt them sexualizing me.. rippin' off my clothes with theirs eyes.. mama say watch what i wear.. my responsibility to make sure grown men don't stare.. i change my clothes but still they stare..

uncles of the family.. whose forceful fingers found their way frolickin' through my forbidden tree.. our family tree tainted by their hands on me.. //

still ain't found freedom to feel free with me.. my own body my greatest liability.. tryna protect this fragile black body in my little black body..

34

most days i fear i can't save my body 'cause i'm trapped inside of me..

they say it must be easy to love my body.. 'cause everybody love my body.. but sometimes i hate my body.. 'cause i can't find me in my body.. because they all had they piece of my body.. this whole world monetized my shape.. i barely see myself in this frame.. flattened to fat ass and flimsy flesh.. this coverin' of my bones always speak for me.. when will my body let **me** speak for me..?[13]

13 "My skin is tan.. My hips invite you..Whose little girl am I? Anyone's.."
Four Women. Nina Simone. Wild Is the Wind. 1996.

PUSSY PLEASURE

first time
i tried
to pleasure me
placing
my pointer finger
up my pussy

i panicked

replayed
scenes in memory
of his pointer finger
up my pussy
pretending
not to notice
pretending
not to panic
normalizing this
nostalgically

first time
i tried
to explore
internal tastes
of my feminine softness
using bare hands
to break through thighs
thawing slimy
squishy content
attempting to embrace

bare boned flesh
i made my vagina
demonic. satanic
hated myself
for touching myself
the way he did

i wanted
to enter me
to calm
the coldened clitoris
inside
clammed up
cried out
choked silent

she couldn't
catch herself
from falling
into hardened hands
of ego
his desire
to control parts of me
i had never known

i tried
to erase
his erection
from the crevices
of my clitoris
to scrape away
his cum stains
from my
sedated girlhood

thought
i could undo
his presence in me
all i could do
was renew
his imprint on me
everytime
i touch me
he still be all i see

...

age thirteen
threw my virginity
to the hounds
like a hop
skip
jump
away from
total consumption

vagina
ripped open
by the hands
of blasphemy
strands of hair
'round clitoris
climbing their way
from freedom
clinging
to the cradled womb
that was girlhood

womanhood
crept up at crevices
of circumcision
demanding
detachment
from youthful innocence

vagina
bled
blue indigo tears
tore open
like laviolette lily
at michigan lake
washed up at shore
of grievances
coral reds
rose golds
gaping
from the gut of her
hanging
off her heartbeat
gasping
for god's green air

...

i was just a girl
gone too soon
experiencing moons of men
too soon

...

i am just a woman
who is still a girl

      every time a man
      cum/
          in me

he still be all i see[14]

---

[14] "To be hot and hard and soft all at the same time.. to feel the deep inside parts of me, sliding and folded and tender and deep."
Lorde, Audre. *Zami: a New Spelling of My Name.* The Crossing Press. 1982.

THIRTY ONE
WRITTEN AT AGE THIRTEEN

i am writing the story of my life
i am writing the story of her life
i am writing the story of our lives
            for truth, for hope, for freedom.

            . . .

i saw the Lord for the first time in a long time
maybe it was a long time
because i kept telling myself
it was the wrong time.
no lie, i knew that if i died that night
i wouldn't see the sky
so why should i waste God's time?
i wasn't ready to change my life of sin
i wasn't ready to make the right decisions

because the sex was good and i liked it
the feeling was strong i couldn't fight it
yet i'd feel so alone when the night ends
just me, myself, and i, no one guidin'
my life too dark to see the light and
my body and soul continue fightin'

after this guy leaves, another one comes
i'd keep 'em coming and cumming
my way of running and shunning
reality, the Lord's been grabbing me
telling me to change but i still stay the same
my soul takes hold of God's grasp

but my body keeps reliving the past

it's no loving just sex, no cares just undress
take me away to that place where i feel sane
but i'm only okay for those few hours
as you devour me, over power me
temporarily fulfill my needs
but when i sleep i often think,

> *will it even be this one next week?*

i see this man in my dreams, this man is a fiend
and me a young queen, thirteen
and he'd say

> *why you got so much booty at this age*
> *so much breast at this age,*
> *girl you don't look yo' age*

that's what this man would say
that's what this fiend would say
that's what he'd say as he'd take my life away

favorite uncle of the family
always came in handy for babysitting
and maybe sitting on the outside looking in
you'd see no sin. that's where his mother was
never believing us, we told her all the time
things just were not right.
but still she left us with him
and he kept us with him,
in his bed under his sheets
full of tears there i'd bleed
stolen virginity
now eighteen years later
still it is he i see in my dreams

they say you grown now, move on now
find a good man and settle down
but i can't settle down with no one

> *lost all my trust in men*
> *can't even hug my own father*

seeing tears from his daughter
caused by his brother
they shared the same mother
but still i deny any kin to him
these men to him are just like me
fiends, doing the same old thing

> *he labeled me a whore at thirteen*

because on that day my dark blue jeans
fit a little too tight and as i tried to fight
he pushed me down and said i was asking for it
so now all i do is keep asking for it
using these men to relive my past
hoping one day i won't see his face as they
overpower me, devour me
temporarily fulfill my needs
and when i sleep i often dream
of the unwritten words
that find courage to speak

> i am writing the story of my life
> i am writing the story of her life
> i am writing, the story of our lives,
> *writing for our collective freedom.*[15]

---

[15] "Broken and bruised, tell me what I am."
Carry Me Home. Jorja Smith. Project 11. 2016.

UNPROTECTED INNOCENCE
FOR REECI BOTTS AND RECY TAYLOR

at thirteen years old, i was re(e)c(i)y-
recy taylor and i shared the same name
            the same story
in 1944
recy stood before an all white jury
in henry county
to testify against her abuser
in 2004
reeci stood before an all white jury
in henry county
to testify against her abuser

in the sixty years between her case and mine
time stood still for black girls like us
unconsented sexual terror
sanctioned by the state
both her abuser and mine walked free

            . . .

trial one, 2003–

it was my first time wearing my hair
natural
new found fluffy fall out curls
flaunting themselves around my ear lobe
lockin' into each other
lovin' on my scalp, effortlessly
my big sister had 'em slicked to the side
wiggled her three fingers through my kitchen

with jam gel, *extra hold*
had my baby hairs swooped and swervin'
just the way i liked 'em

the jury didn't like 'em
the contagious kinks
crinkled on top of my untamable mane
because baby hairs made brown baby girls
look like they grew up too
fast, fresh, freaky, fornicatin'
fuckin' for food and clothes
the way i wore natural hair on my forehead
made me look like not thirteen years old
like not deserving protection

the jury was hung
and i damn near hung
my girlhood with a noose
to the magnolia tree that day
outside the courtroom, i could hear them say
>*she doesn't look her age*
>*she doesn't look her age*

trial two, 2004–

it was my first time wearing my hair
pressed
curled
sheened
glossed
bouncin' its own two step to the step of my stroll
with a brainwashed, head tossed
mind of its own
kinky curls pressed straight
into america's framework of femininity

my big sister ain't know how to press or curl
mama said she wasn't allowed
to lay jam gel swirls to my edges no more
mama told sista tee from church
to fix her baby's hair for the next court date
so i could look professional for the white folk
mama took me shopping at macy's
for a two piece suit and penny loafer shoes
so i could look respectable for the white folk

//

in 2003, the jury was hung
and my innocence was hung
with a noose to the oak tree that day
mama hung head low
longing for leveraging tools
to protect her baby from this man
   this system

but there was no slippin' my size six thighs
into a proper performance of innocence
the jury would never like me
the way my ass
filled out a houndstooth pencil skirt
the way my breasts
cupped a white button down shirt

my abuser was found innocent
because the jury could not see innocence
between the three fingered waves
my big sister styled across my forehead
because my body shaped a suit like a
woman

because girls like me cannot be raped
only tamed, only shamed, only blamed

1944 – 2004

rest in peace to the innocence of girls
who have ever been *re(e)c(i)y* in their lifetime
who were too black and too bold
for a henry county courtroom
whose innocence was stolen by a man
whose innocence was protected by the law
rest in peace
to girls with black girlhoods like ours
who never found protection in innocence[16]

---

[16] "This racialized formulation of gender and class – sexually promiscuous young girls,
turned into irresponsible young.. women.. – can flourish in part because in many cases no
one – no friend, family member, or advocate, no official representative from the state, and
no reporter – asks about these young women's lives.. [No one asked how] she could be
repeatedly raped by her uncle, under her boyfriend's constant surveillance, and terrified of
her family or community's response."
Riche, Beth E. *Arrested Justice: Black Women, Violence, and America's Prison Nation.* New York
University Press. 2012.

BEYOND CURVES
FOR SARAH BAARTMAN
"HOTTENTOT VENUS"

some days
when i stare
at my curves

i see sarah
and wonder
how she felt
about herself

how objectified
ass and titties
take a toll on a
black woman's soul
on spiritual beauty, on
The Light

when waist slim
hips wide
Coca-Cola back arch
'cause black arch
naturally

no ass shots
or kanye workout plan
she ain't workin out a plan
to get through life
free 99
no, she is worked
for free 99

her worth
belittled
to a dollar sign
nickeled and dimed
pinned up property

so excuse me
if i am mistaken
but your mistaken
interpretation
of my womanhood
feels too much like
south african afrikkkaners
tellin' black african women

> body is beauty
> booty is beauty
> behold
> a brown girl
> whose body is benevolent
> who is nothing but body
> handcrafted for male pleasure

since
all i could ever be
is out my element
in a world that deems curves
the sole measurement
of my being

.

some days
when i stare
in the mirror
jumping my curves into

fitted boot length Levi jean
jammin' to Jamaican Funk
feelin free as forever

      then frozen.
how quickly i forget
the rules of this
thick girl game

> *sexy or safety*
> *sensuality or sanity*

how quickly i forget
the last time i lingered
in flashing lights
of los angeles

men assumed
my shape
was longing
for their attention
dimensions
of my waistline
assline
hipline
on display
dared to wear
dazzled dress
dipped low in front
hugged tight in back
back out
breasts out
shape out

piercing eyes
played
in my promised land
placed
puzzling hands
in holy places
pretended
they belonged there
situated
bodies on my body
barricaded
my breasts into bar
bickered over whose bills
would buy me out

outside the bar
blending bodies
meet and beat a two step
to step in the name of love
but when a brown girl
don't consent
to that song
to that dance
the beat keep blastin
the bar keep bumpin

the bass bombards her

blowing her body
back in the wind
      bitch, you better back dat fat ass up

barely bold enough to behave
battling internal borderlands
basing beauty on they dollar signs

singing along with Beyonce
barely breathing
bitch, you better back dat fat ass up

i couldn't even lie and say
i ain't sorry
because i was sorry
because i was a brown girl
with too much body
who never wanted to be
ashamed of a shape
that shifts their expectations
but men have ways
of silencing freedom
when you look like me
you must be tamed

.

some days
when i stare in the mirror
i hear my mother's voice
in my ear
> *cover up blackgirl,*
> *all that body*
> *cover up blackgirl*
> *you got too much body*

some days
i strip down to nothing
nod my head
bend neck low
and lie to me
allow myself to believe
that knee length sweaters
and large size coats

could cover up
the capacity of my curves
that my favorite fitted Levi jeans
should've been left at Lenox on layaway
i let them label me
let them lie to me
let their limited conceptions
of my character
caution me
'cause the less they see
the more they'll see[17]

[17] "Big ol' ass. Big ol' tits. (She's a baby, baby, baby). She so big. Won't nobody even try to reach her mind.. Won't stop to recognize that there's more, more underneath that thickness."
Jill Scott. *Thickness*. Experience: Jill Scott 826+. 2001.

EROTIC

when you
simmer in steam shower
heat trickling down
bare boned body

when you
touch yourself,
hug yourself,
love yourself
rub
bathroom mirror fog
to see
yourself
fall back into arms
of self
sis, that is a
freedom

when you
caress
your own breasts
squeeze
your own hips
touch
your own thighs

and know

that power lies
within.
between.
below.

know that

arodecent prisms
birthed in your womb
nurtured in your bosom
collided other worlds
inside you

when you
lay unclothed
in garden of gardenia
resting your uterus
at the edge of earth
when you
touch yourself
hug yourself
love yourself
look deep into moon
to see yourself
fall back in love
with self

and know

the true pleasure
of your pussy
is the orgasmic
self summoning
that erupts
from the darkest place
within you
baby girl
that is liberation[18]

---

18 "The erotic is a resource within each of us that lies in a deeply female and spiritual plane, firmly rooted in the power of our unexpressed or unrecognized feeling."
Lorde, Audre. *Sister Outsider: Essays and Speeches*: *Uses of the Erotic: The Erotic as Power*. Trumansburg, NY: Crossing Press, 1984.

ANCESTRAL GRIEVING

before i knew my self, i knew my ancestry.. the black women who came before me made their presence known in me.. at age thirteen, for my eighth grade project on black women poets of the past / present / future, nzadi told her story through me.. that's when i knew that she and her forgotten daughters had never forgotten me..

at age thirteen, i sat on the edge of my bed and transitioned beyond the edge of an astral plane between a present pennsylvania and a west african past.. for twenty three minutes i wrote from that place.. like a well of water flowing from the fountain of my foremothers, i wrote.. like a child with a woman inside her, i wrote.. like a little old soul seeking language untold, i wrote and i wrote and i wrote.. revealing a revolution inside me.. reliving a ritualistic rites of passage that birthed itself inside the slave ship.. this pen and pad a spaceship of site and sound that transported me back in time to see motions of oceans that drowned nzadi's first born baby girl.. gone too soon, grown too soon, like me.. saw the sun in the moon until the morning after her rape forced her astray, like me.. until her black girlhood made her black woman, like me..

uprooted by intrusions of the truest form of life known to humankind.. the black woman's mind and memory of a time that was taken from us.. a time we now reclaim.. at thirteen i reclaimed a recollection of a reflection of my self.. unaware of what words had come from some deep source in me, i followed the orders of those foremothers and let the paper and pen be the archive for the pouring out of their memory.. thus, nzadi became my entry to self knowing..

at age twenty three i looked out over cape coast and cradled my own wounds.. west africa no longer a distant memory, but a part of me.. a home that engulfed me physically.. it hurt and healed and hurt and healed.. the deep drowning i felt after placing one foot before the other beneath the dungeon of darkness where they held my dearest nzadi.. the haunted history of these heinous crimes against the black women who birthed me.. in ghana, i gained clarity of this fact - that my people were never 'pose to go back.. but there i was, returning, for all nzadi's daughters who never could.. //

at twenty three o'clock in the midnight moon i made my eyes shut
just long enough to stop seeing the ghosts of the past i left behind..
black womb banging on my windows.. woman with weary heart and
unsettled spirit showed herself in me.. sank deeper into the frail of my
skin.. showed her truth in my truth and dared me to deny her presence..
i prayed for peace.. prayed for protection.. prayed for her to pass me by..
but she refused to leave me alone and God let her live with me, even just
for the night.. in the city of the jazz that justifies my soul, i sank into
white silk sheets in black dress at my funeral.. felt the stench of her death
at my doorstep.. skulls i could not escape.. fate i could not escape.. faith i
could not fake.. forced to free myself when no one else was around.. alone
in old city, new orleans.. knowing in that moment i was not alone, was
not home, was haunted by remnants of unspoken mysteries..

a wise woman told me that i must always win peace through love.. that
no entity is ever my enemy.. that demons never existed.. that healed and
unhealed souls sit in the cracks of the walls of hotel rooms and haunt
the wandering bodies that breathe life into the spaces that were once
forgotten.. that if the sound of my spirit always vibrates high enough
to heal my own heart, then i will always find pieces of power within
me.. and that word from that wise woman on that worry filled morning
settled me.. in that moment, the mirrors and the motions all mocking
me, i had nothing left to do but channel the choir of my depths and dig
out from my darkness the intensity of the love of God in me..

//

today, i sit beneath georgia oak trees.. making meaning of my existence..
connecting with ancestors whose spirits sing my sorrows.. they continue
to guide my quest through the universe.. i trace my mama all the way
back to ghana in my imagination.. mama, whose mama was creole and
cajun.. geechee and gulluh.. south carolina and louisiana.. enslaved and
free.. whose mama's mama survived for the possibility of me.. the women
who lived and died to imagine me care free.. the women whose torture
and triumph paved the way for my own.. the memory of grannie mamie

and ethel mae jolt me back to a day when women who were black and
bold faced death.. feared life.. yet lived, still, unashamed of all God made
them..[19]

---

19 "Black butterfly, sail across the waters. Tell your..daughters what the struggle brings."
Black Butterfly. Denise Williams. Let's Hear it for the Boy. 1984.

AFRICA
WRITTEN AT AGE THIRTEEN

my name is Nzadi of Ghana, West Africa
where the sun shines bright
and reflects off the seas
and the trees only sway one way

yet that breeze on a Sunday
couldn't cure a runaway
from her heartache and pain
'cause when the white man
and his right hand
slapped a white rope down on us black folks
they labeled us niggas and shipped us
off to America. locked us up in gates
and proclaimed their hate
for our kind
but why couldn't they find
the beauty from within
our dark brown skin

back then
my baby girl was only thirteen
beautiful chocolate cream
but as she began to scream
our being became unseen
and as her tears began to multiply
our names became undefined
our roots began to get lost in the soil
and our recollection of Africa began to spoil

they made us lose pride in our homes
they forced us to sing this sad song now
and move on now
we try to stay strong now
but the white man keep bringing us down

its freedom that we had
its freedom we've been deprived of
we try to rise up
but the white man keep
oppressing us, depressing us
and bringing us down
and bringing our young black females down
the crown is only worn by the beholder
and she told him
you are not the God of anything
especially not me

but that was only on the first day
'cause the next day
she learned to keep her mouth shut
before she get fucked up
like the rest of them
look at the breast of them
been touched on so many times
feels like they can't even cry no more
look to the sky some more
but God feels like nothing
'cause every time they mourn
it's like,

> *God can you hear me ?*
> *why can't you stay near me*
> *done cried so many tears see*
> *it's like nothing's left*

>   *and the best of me was left*
>   *back in Africa*

and she cried because he raped her
then i'd cry because i could not save her
i allowed him to rename her
a nigger wench, just a teenager
never asked for no favors
just asked for her to make it
through this life of hatred
God it is for her that I pray
and maybe one day
you can send her back to that place
where the sun shines bright
and reflects off the seas
and the trees only sway one way
and let that breeze on a Sunday
cure my baby girl's pain
and no matter what others may say
let Africa, remain her name
>   let Africa, remain her name
>   *Lord, let Africa always remain our name.*[20]

---

20 "No longer able to recall the shrines or sacred groves or water deities or ancestor
spirits.. She was defenseless. No longer anyone's child."
Hartman, Saidiya. *Lose your mother: a Journey Along the Atlantic Slave Route*. New York: Farrar,
Straus and Giroux, 2007.

PRETTY LITTLE FOOL

bare as the day i was born
birthed in the basement of black
back bathed in holy water

mama prayed for pretty little fool
never wanted baby girl
to know the world like she
       cruel and **unforgiving**[21]

---

[21] "My mother was a blind architect. Her mother was too.. Born with a brick heart and mortar tongue, they made due. Now the only thing I know is to build those same walls too."
Fragile. Eryn Allen Kane. a tree planted by water. 2019.

MUSIC OUR MOTHERS CRIED TO

my mother
cried
to anita baker

her mother
cried
to ms simone

her mother
cried
to gladys
and the pips
starin out
windows
alone

i
cry
to every
woman
all the
women
of my
bloodline
do

and
my
unborn
daughter,

dancin
slow jazz
in heaven,
yea
she do
too[22]

---

[22] "I keep wondering what I'm gonna do without you."
Neither One of Us. Gladys Knight and the Pips. 1973.

A CONJURING OF MAIDEN NAMES

LaViolette
rolls off
tongues
like cursive

gel pens paint
l shaped glory
onto lineless page
spellin' out *love*
in childhood
diaries
as if
blackgirl
ever knew
its meaning

LaViolette
rolls off
tongues
like romance
like first dance
like my mother's
highschool
sweetheart

1979. prom
pageant
homecoming
ball game
light washed
vintage levi jeans

LaViolette
means things
to my mother
LaViolette
means things
to me

LaViolette
rolls off
tongues
like speakin'
in tongues
like lillies
laid out 'cross
dining room
table
dipped in
holy water
drenched
in gold

LaViolette
rolls off
tongues
like creoles
of La Plaz
like Louisiana
poboys
like memories
lost
longed for
made up
like
fictive kin

Botts
breaks down
the flow
of things
bulky
ugly
chunky
clunky
thick
between
yo teeth

Botts be
daddy's
daddy
drinkin'
beatin'
ethel mae

Botts be
darkness
clouded
by shame
silence
secrets
untold
childhoods
forgotten

Botts
be burden
Botts
be baggage
Botts
be weight

LaViolette
be dainty
delicacy
doodled
pansies
potpourri
planted seeds
sunshined
blue skied
kisses on
yo cheek
be neon
crop tops
and afro sheen

LaViolette
be high yella
got a fella
old school
beauty
urban chic
sunday swing
jammer seven
roller rink
motown
at sun down
detroit red
detroit bred
detroit fed
be nostalgia
for a time
my mother
came alive in
a longing
for the city
that grew her

Botts
be the
patriarchy
that suffocated
LaViolette

Botts be
country
uncomfy
chunky
clunky
heavy
on the tongue
heavy
on the heart

>   *but*
>   *i have*
>   *never*
>   *known*
>   *myself*
>   *any*
>   *other*
>   *way*

Botts
carry
my
stench
my
sin
my
soliloquy

i hate how
hardening

it feels
on my
tongue
but
it is my father's
and it is mine

. . .

brittany botts
be the name
they gave to me

ree botts
be the name
i made for me

i let me
reemake
me over

~~ree botts~~

~~ree ward~~

~~ree LaViolette botts~~

~~ree LaViolette ward~~

reelaviolette *botts-ward*

i am
somebody's
wife now

ward
will not
be my
undoing

botts was
my mother's
undoing

laviolette
was her mother's
undoing

sibert
was her mother's
undoing

reelaviolette botts-ward

my name
_ree_claims
laviolette

it will
not be my
undoing

my name
a secret
attempt to
put mama
back together

but she is
already
undone

. . .

i romanticize
LaViolette
as my mother
romanticizes
herself
to me

sometimes
pretty words
hide pain
real good
sometimes
pretty names
mask shame
real good
sometimes
pretty letters
be in vain
sometimes
pretty women
think
pretty women
are to blame

my
mother's
mother
swallowed

whole
by the
same
name
i cling to

LaViolette
be baggage
LaViolette
be weight
LaViolette
be trauma
that look like
sunshine

but it
too
is mine
it's mine
it is my mother's
and it is mine

...

every
generation
of woman
in my
bloodline
mourns
the name
of her
girlhood
as she

passes
down
his
name
to
her
daughters

there were only ever
daughters
there are no more
laviolettes

. . .

my name
will make
warriors
of the
women
who legacy
forgot

of botts
of sibert
of laviolette

MY MOTHER'S GARDEN

so what might i find in my mother's garden?
dusted records of Jackson 5 and Funkadelics.
golden crochet sticks and purple yarn.
preteen newspaper scrapings
from miscellaneous anecdotes
of a girlhood she still clings to.
yearning.
longing.
desire.
distress.

what might i find in my mother's garden?
the same stuff that's inside me.
loss.
pain.
fear.
defeat.
silence.
stillness.
discomfort.

what might i find in the garden of my mother,
the mother who has forgotten me -
a glow.
a note.
a poem written in a journal beneath her bed.
no lock.
trusting us not to peek.
peace.
pieces of herself fragmented across pansies.
pieces of me.

. . .

my mother's garden is guarded.
yet i know the landscape of her floral footprint
like the lilacs of my own.
how might i have access
to the intricacies of her garden
 if she never let me in?

i feel the fruit of her forest
in the ripples of my own
i sucked the nectar from her nipples as a babe
and never forgot how it tasted

my mother, like Alice's mother,
adorns the interiority of her soul
with sunflowers
even when the sun don't shine.
sometimes, i would see storm in her eyes
but she never let those sunflowers die.
tried her best to tend to her garden,
gauging the amount of water her soil needed,
not always knowing her boundaries
when she was depleted

she never learned how to balance
mourning with levity
i hope that i am learning for her.[23]

23 "In search of my mother's garden, I found my own."
Walker, Alice. *In Search of Our Mothers' Gardens.* Harcourt. 1983.

FREEDOM'S DAUGHTER

i am the daughter
of Freedom
her last born soliloquy
yes, i am Freedom's daughter
and no one else's

i used to be an orphan
with motherless tales
and fatherless anecdotes
with holes forming in spaces
where i wished to be most whole

and then i was reborn
in a field of my
fragmented fairy tales
with unicorn blessings
in babylon birthings

i remet the man i once knew
and learned of his hatred for me
it was my freedom that harmed him
scared him away
haunted him like haints
in his high yella nightmares
he hated to see
the grandchild of Ethel Mae
so fucking untamed

.

i holler and scream
when he hits me
when his hands crack my hip
when his fists grip
my senegalese twists
when i twist and turn
because i will never learn
to submit

.

submissive women
servant women
deserving service
women who rarely sit
to sip soup and tea
(honey suckled scent)
women who repent
for the sins of men
who harmed them

owing the entirety
of her existence
to a love song
sorrowful
singing sorries
in sickening melodies
believing
the woman was always
to blame

but i will never be her
because i am Freedom's daughter
and mama raised me different

.

my truth
forces him to remember
all the ugliest parts
of himself

he screams
>*stop shaking*
>*stop faking your own death*

as if
when you trace my skin
like scales of a fish
you won't find scars
he left behind

scars that wash their cum
on my canvas
cake their insecurities
between my bronzer and mascara
numb. nauseous. nibbling at my tit
finding comfort in the
carving out of womb

i scream

>*i am never tied to nothin'*
>*not even you*
>*i abide by my own necessity*
>*you are no necessity*
>*need sesame seeds*
>*and palms trees*
>*sunflowers*
>*and saged beads*
>*but i will never need*
>*you*
>*that is why you hate me*
>*so much*

i
wild as wind and wolves
am
the daughter of
Freedom
and will never be
the daughter
of man[24]

---

24 "Wild women, they fly free.. Wild women are not to be tamed, only admired."
Wild Women. Sunni Patterson. 2019.

SEQUOIA

trace sequoia root
as i trace my own
foundation

of her trunk
coiled up
remind me of
mama
remind me of

all the black hair i love
of church ladies
with dancing locs
that look like curly fries

the fires she fought
fearless
remind me
of great grandmama
of grenada
of black womanhood

.

vagina shaped holes
unhealed
revealed
in her nakedness
exposed

what if sequoia
ain't want the world
to know
between her thighs?

remind me of bodies
black and female
and always on display
like mama
and grandmama
and church ladies
and me
why we can't never hide
how the world
damage our insides?

sequoia
no longer
moans and mourns
no longer
longs to be hidden
covered. tucked away
behind her mother's home
to heal in peace
in privacy

she has learned
to love every inch
of the body
that is left of her

.

            my spirit floats to her
            my soul cries for her
            she cries for me, too

loudly

yet all is still and silent and well

> *i see you*
> *i hear you*
> *i feel you*

i no longer fear
the spirit
i let it summon me
into her forest

i echo her song

> *i see you*
> *i hear you*
> *i feel you*

.

sequoia
narrates stories
about women
who survive fires
who show their scars
to the world
inspire vulnerability
how the openness
of her gauges
the holes in the center
of her heart
hypervisible
to those passersby
yet the tree mothers
do not hide

do not hang head low
embarrassed
of the wounds
from their womb

> even in your death
> you produce life
> even in the wake
> of your womb
> you birth light
> your roots rise to skies
> unknown to man
> to carve an opening
> for healing

she points
to the crevice
of her hip
where fire
burned flesh
where beetle
bit through breasts
where forest
could not protect

what remained of her
was raw and real
what remained of her
resembled me
the insides of my core
that i cannot reach
the parts of me
i be too scared to see
the tree
is not afraid of me
she is not suspicious

of my longing

she teaches me
to struggle
and still stand
one thousand feet tall
one thousand years long
touching blues of skies
like we deserve to
like the rape of our nation
the slitting of our tongues
the stripping of our skin
the burning of our flesh
could never really break us
could never really kill us
for even if one of us fall
fields of our foremothers
grow fortified
in imaginaries of
black feminist futures

.

.

.

we mirror our hair
after tree mothers
the coiled kinks that
spin themselves
into dance formations
atop a black girl's mane
like the twisted roots
of the sequoia

we mirror our mourning
after tree mothers
our menstruation
after the shedding of leaves
our love
after the kissing
of queen-sized redwoods
reuniting
ninety thousand feet
above ground
branches
bursting into lullabied song
pushed between
each other's trunk
don't quite know
where one ends
and the other begins

we mirror our care
after tree mothers
brown skin
in synch
with hers
here in these backwoods
of California
enclaves of communal nurturing
of thousand year old trees
who survived everything[25]

---

[25] I close my eyes and I am in the forest with sequoia whenever this song plays. *Sacred Bath*. Destiny Muhammed. Sacred Bath. 2007.

THE EAGLE IN MY SKY

a woman
i once knew
reimagined herself
black satin silk
saw self
in mirror image
of holy
claimed sanctity
prior to surname
untamed
a tamed mind
freed
a captured spirit
blossomed
into Eagle
soaring
far above the cloud
on which i still lay
and dream
about the Eagles
above me
wondering
which one she became[26]

26 "Dancing on the astral plane, holy water cleansing rain, floating through the stratosphere."
Astral Plane. Valerie June. The Order of Time. 2017.

BLACK (W)HOLES

me
a Black woman
who is a Black hole
holds close
everything that is sacred

me
a Black hole
who is a mother
to myself
holds close
everything that is
chaotic. floating.
like frictioned galaxies
that escape my
slit of wrist

me
a Black girl
gone wrong
holds close
the Black hole
of a womb
that ruptures
each time
i take me home

me
whose unhealed holes
made her not know
her

self
me
with each Black hole
in my heart
with each Black
scar that scrapes my throat

me
a Black girl
who is also
a Black hole
who be stuck
in the hold
of the wake[27]

me
who have no map
to make sense of

me
a whole ass
Black girl womanchild[28]
womb of the wake
wanderin soul
me
who sense somethin
greater than flesh
in spirit

me
a collection

[27] Sharp, Christina. *In the Wake: on Blackness and Being*. Duke University Press. Duke University Press. 2016.

28 Shange, Savannah. Black Girl Ordinary: Flesh, Carcerality and the Refusal of Ethnography. *Transforming Anthropology Vol 27*.

of Black holes
a curation
of the unclothed
a citation
of bare boned
naked
nude
unnurtured
holes
in every single
Black girl womanchild
i know

me
a mosaic of all the
unwhole folks
who claim Black and womb
by they surname
me
a compilation
of catastrophe
an exhibition
of the catastrophic
Eurosphere
that forced me into
Black holes

me
who is hurtin
from all those holes

me
a skin cell
me

an inkwell[29]
me
unwatered
me
a plucking
out a root
me
a floating
with no shoes
a feather
with no grounding

me
a moment of
collapse
in space/ time
a sinking
into my own
Black hole
with hopes
of comin back
whole

me
a hand full
of honey
a hair strand
of kink
a cloth patterned

---

29 The Inkwell is a term that refers to the only portion of Martha's Vineyard where Black folks were allowed to be when the vacation spot was legally segregated. What was initially a derogatory term became a stomping grounds for Black creatives to convene and exchange their art. Peters, Donna-Marie. *Inked: historic African-American beach site as collective memory and group 'Third Place' sociability on Martha's Vineyard.* Leisure Studies, Volume 35. Pages 187-199 | Received 07 Jan 2014, Accepted 23 Sep 2014, Published online: 27 Nov 2014.

with memory
a gourd
made for drinkin
a psalm and a jazz
made for thinkin

me
and all the things
i never knew
to love
float into the abyss of
me

me
and the combination
of every Black hole
i own
rupture
a myth of bliss
we become
unknown to ourselves
a satan waitin' to bloom

//

soon,
Black hole
you will learn
how you survived
how you climbed
yourself
outside yourself
right before your moon

soon,
Blackgirl,

you will learn
the love
of mystic darkness[30]
is what saved you
the sacred
of her covering
the care
of her hold
on you
how she suck
you in
make you stuck
with sin
just so you
could return
to you

soon,
you yearning
mourning
breathing
Black hole
you
Black womanchild[31]
will thank
your womb
for rebirthing you[32]
for renaming
your Black hole

30 Malika Imhotep, Ra and baker, miyuki. *The Black Feminist Study Theory Atlas,* The Church of Black Feminist Thought. 2019. (17)

31 Shange, Savannah. Black Girl Ordinary: Flesh, Carcerality and the Refusal of Ethnography. *Transforming Anthropology Vol 27.*

32 Alexander, Jacqui M. *Pedagogies of Crossing: Meditations on Feminism, Sedual Politics, Memory and the Sacred,* Duke University Press. (270)

whole
holder
of all that is sacred
releaser
of all that has wings
that which can afford
to fly from you
and find home
in someone else's

soon,
my child,
you will see
that there could be
no growth
beyond Black holes
that journeying deeper
into some soil
is the only way
to work
with yo hands
to heal the holes
who summon you

soon,
someone will say
something about a hatred
for darkness
and you will understand it
as an anti-God
a hatred for holes
a refusing of whole[33]

---

[33]Malika Imhotep, Ra and baker, miyuki. *The Black Feminist Study Theory Atlas,* The Church of Black Feminist Thought. 2019.

soon,
you will realize
that Black girls
with holes
all learned
to disguise themselves
as you

soon,
you will see
in the learning
of your womb
that darkness
always brings truth[34]

---

34 "Moving out of the twilight can also mean moving into the dark, which sometimes is where the true light exists. The sun is always there, just obliterated under a cloud of dark grayness, ready to be revealed if one could only burst through and penetrate the surface obscurity."

Davies, Carole Boyce. *Caribbean Spaces: Escapes from Twilight Zones.* Champaign: University of Illinois Press, 2013. (23)

HEALING AT HOME:
A LOVE LETTER TO BLACKGIRL
SANCTUARY

I.

you started as a blank canvas
uncurated
uncultivated
uncushioned
quiet
squeaks of your hinges haunted me
hardwood floors felt cold and callous
cutting through the thick of my skin
beneath my feet

frustrated,

i couldn't read you
i couldn't reach you
yearning for some form of recognition
from you
to see me and set me free
here
lay me to rest in the rawness of your warmth
i saw potential in you
past the painful sleepless nights you caused
crying babies out my window
crack babies out my window
cracks in the paint at my window
can't see the sun out my window
cried in my baby's arms
as i stared out the window

of this strange widowed place
that felt as vacant as my heart
yet from here
is where we created *art*...

//

on move in day
in order to keep sane
i decorated.
decorated every inch of every corner
placed petals of dead flowers
in the cracks of your crevices
just to remind myself
there is life after death,
there is life after death
carried couches and chairs
down east oakland sidewalks
to make you my sanctuary
to shelter myself from you, in you, with you
you would become who i needed you to
cause i needed you to
be it one week or two or three
i would make a home of you

//

i made my way through life through you
the day i declared.
i dared face the darkness you held
in the hollowness of your heroes
whose honest scent lingered behind
like a black widow in her wilderness
whose blood still boldly buried beneath your concrete
i could feel her fumbling in my garden when i'd sleep
i sent for you

but had to go through her first

and she never feared me
until i remembered that i must not fear her
she was the wicked of the past i left behind
she was a reflection of the darkness in me

//

that day at the meditation center
alice walker reminded me
with her soft hands and calm smile
embracing me carefully
"you have the power, sister"

the power to cultivate a garden
to pull from the powers of my mothers
to pull from the depths of the dirt
and dig out the gem
to know that light always wins
and i will always be light so long as i choose
and now i am light
and now you are light too.

II.

you
physical space of sage and scents
you who ignites metaphysical space
inside my inner place
of sage and scents
you are the light that reflects my light
so i must never fear you
even when i fear me
even when i can't face myself
you give me space to embrace myself

the booty shakin
book reading
journal writing
red lip rockin
poet
scholar
activist
and you let me be
all of these things
all at once
with no pressure to compartmentalize
in a world that demands i compartmentalize
you are the only place in the world
where my world is my own
you let me walk into my world
with my name on it

you let me be
thirteen year old ree
playin
patty-cake-pick-a-boo-little-Sally Walker
you let me wonder what life might be like
if this world loved black women
because in this alternate universe
that you and i create
this world loves black women
like me
with my tongue out and my thighs out
in my two tone
red bone
high yella skin
home is here
healing is here
you cultivate home inside me

III.

my sacred sanctuary of healing
you see me in all of my rawness
and you love me most here
in the darkest part
of my deepest dungeon
where the demons live and lurk
you meet me here
and embrace me here
and remind me that i am

Holy

with my ashy knees
and sheabutterless, uncreamed,
coiled, kinky hair
frizzed and napped
the kitchen at the nape of my neck
collecting dust
cause i'm depressed
and dry
and stale
and lonely
but you see me
and you seek me
and you reflect me

//

during the holidays
when i ain't have no family
you was my family
tucked me in extra tight that night
and nestled me into your warmth
you helped me trim the tree
and tie the bow in a knot
draped the lights across each branch

hung the stockings and danced with me
to all my favorite nostalgic slow jams
like This Christmas and Jackson 5's
santa kissing mama under the mistletoe
and on the part when Michael come in and say
"no, no I really *did* see mommy kissin' santa clause"
when i recited every word
you didn't even laugh at me
you just let me be
weird and quirky and crazy in my own way

you knew that's the song i use to sing with mama
and you comforted me for my loss
you let me laugh at myself
and love
and grieve
and get better
and get worse
and get restless
and retreat
and retrieve
and conspire to kick myself out my own world
when i become too much for me

but when i wanna return
you always welcome me back
with open arms
no harm ever done

IV.

some say you are but a figment of my imagination
but i once imagined you
at a time when i struggled to imagine myself
and you became reality
and i retained reality

many may not believe in your power
but your power is simply the power within me
reflected back to me
reflections of myself at every angle i turn
you become the depiction of my highest me

a memory of ancient black motherhood
that always birthed green
always planted seeds
out flower pots surrounded by poisonous weeds
the slave mama
who always made somethin out of nothin
the poor mama
whose hands danced away poverty
with sprouting tulips and purple pansies
who never had a lot but always had a home
who turned a hut into a home
who made space to belong

//

and don't every black woman deserve this,
a space she can call her sanctuary?
to sit still in her magic
and make meaning of her life
to let her truth form before her
to cultivate the vacant space inside her heart
where art is awaiting creation
where her ritual of righting wrongs and singing songs off key in her
shower can occur
a place where her life can occur

where do black women go
when life lets us down?
we go home
and shouldn't our homes

be spaces of healing,
if nowhere else in this world
will be?

to kneel at our altars
and pray to our ancestors
and rejoice to our gods
and give grace to our enemies
and meditate away negative energies
and embrace positivity
don't we deserve that space?

yes we go home
to heal
we find home inside a little lot of land
where we proudly place our name and say
i curate my healing here
i escape here
and that little plot of pain in our hearts
ceases its tension
even just for a moment...[35]

---

[35] "You see me in all of my rawness and you love me most here."
Healing at Home: an Ode to Black Girl Sanctuary. Ree Botts. 2018.

www.blackwomxnhealing.com

CLASSROOM GUIDE

this book is written in conversation with my dissertation project, which merges radical black feminist methodologies with womanist artistry to explore curations of black women's healing spaces in oakland. as a doctoral candidate at the university of california, berkeley, i have spent the past five years witnessing black women in intimate moments of communal care and self recovery. this project forced me deeper into myself. my journey inward birthed the content of this book.

A NOTE ON BLACKGIRL PEDAGOGY

as an educator, i ground my teaching in an *everyday round the way blackgirl pedagogy*, a method of engagement that affirms the ghetto as sacred and the sacred as ghetto. as a woman whose inner[blackgirl] child is both hood and prolific, ratchet and profound, i make space for students to be multifaceted. i merge collective narratives of everyday blackgirl life with black feminist care and womanist praxis. we place the beauty supply store in conversation with ancestral astral planes, via alice walker and audre lorde, and we theorize from that place. we center our creative process as the most rigorous site of our analysis.

.

i invite my students out of head space and into heart space, and i invite you to do the same. allow yourself and your students to feel my words with your spirit, for this is the purest way to witness my inner[blackgirl]child, and to witness your own.

A RITUAL FOR TEACHING

.

one

situate this work as a theoretical intervention into black women's studies and black girlhood studies. this is a book about inner child healing for black women still learning to love the little blackgirl within. very little has been written on black women's processes of healing inner child trauma, particularly as folks who experience the weight of our gendered and racialized im/possibilities. the ways race denotes gender, preventing access to girlhood/ womanhood/ innocence, is the root of many black women's deepest childhood wounds. inspired by the twelve steps of aca, where folks experience spiritual awakening through the reclamation of the inner child, i work to expand the framework of inner child healing to center the relationship between black women and our own girlhoods, with a focus on grieving the losses we never learned to name.

.

two

read alongside blackwomxnhealing.com/book. use multimedia blackgirl artistry to guide your collective experience. invite students to explore the list of sources cited in each footnote. discuss:

what do these black womxn artists have to say about black girlhood.. black womxnhood.. ancestry.. healing.. selfhood.. spirituality.. ?

allow students to create their own multi-medium art piece inspired by these black feminists' creative works. lean into paint.. color.. sound.. collage.. let students be as creative as they want to be.

.

three

guide students in a grounding meditation. breathe deep.. collectively.. invite students into the body.. into themselves.. invite them to convene with their inner[blackgirl]child.

> *suggested meditation script*
>
> as we center ourselves into our bodies.. becoming aware of our breath.. expanding our hearts, minds, and spirits to receive the blessing of our inner selves.. i want you to picture your younger self.. what does she look like? what is she wearing? take a moment to witness her in her fullness.. what is she doing? how does she feel? allow your adult self to hug your little self as you breathe life.. love.. and affirmation into her.. let her know you are here to protect her.. that you are journeying home into yourself to give her all the care and comfort she deserves..

.

four

invite students to write a love letter to their inner[blackgirl]child.

.

five

invite students' inner[blackgirl]child to respond.. using the non dominant hand, and whatever art supplies the inner child desires, respond to the love letter with words, images, colors, art - in whatever way the inner child desires. allow the child to be free to create with no bounds. let it be unneat. let her show up however she wants to in the moment. do not censor, do not judge..

AN OFFERING

for toni brown... my first poetry mentor at age thirteen, with whom this book project began... thank you for taking your time with me... for meeting me on weekends at barnes n nobles and telling me my poetry was worthy... thank you for watching over me... for giving me my first copy of *for colored girls*, from which i still teach... thank you for teaching me to "[find] god in myself and... [to] love her fiercely...[1]" thank you for those words on your obituary... for your audacity to affirm that god lived within a black woman like you... like me... i know your soul is resting in clouds of poetry... thank you for still reminding me you're proud of me...

for my dream girls... my mother and sister... who always believed in my light and cheered me on every step of the way... whose support for me made me believe in endless possibilities... who know my heart and see my pain and inspire me to my purpose... who continue to love me unconditionally even when i grew... who hold me close the best ways they know how throughout my process of healing...

for osceola ward... who in my lowest moment gifted me with the inner child healing book that birthed my quest for britt britt... whose commitment to his own healing invited me deeper into my own... the man who teaches me new ways to love myself by the way he loves me... who showed me my reflection in nature and nurtures my tender wounds... who is fragile with my faith and careful with my heart... who makes me feel free as yellow flowers... thank you for being britt britt's bestest friend... for being my mirror into all my dark parts... for making all this space for me to grow...

---

[1]Shange, Ntozake. *For Colored Girls Who Have Considered Suicide / When the Rainbow Is Enuf.* Scribner Poetry. 1975.

for brianna baker... baby speshy, whose commitment to the liberation of blackgirls inspires my own... who has been fully present at every stage of my adulthood transformation to put life in perspective... who finds joy in my success and teaches lessons in the midst of perceived failures... who makes space for all my spirit dreams and lets me process the complexities of what purpose means to me... who illustrates for me what true sisterhood feels like...

for brax... you invite me so deeply into myself... to sit with what is scary... to mend the deepest wounds... you see me in my darkness and reflect me back to me...

.

brax was unafraid to discover her inner[blackgirl]child... she welcomed Little Brax into her womxnhood and allowed her to be a spirit guide in the process of healing... the places braxton journeyed to inside herself brought peace... joy... levity... those places also revealed layers of heaviness and grief...brax was so brave and so bold in her commitment to being whole that she let herself travel into that darkness, unafraid to move through looming corners of her interior to locate what was still bleeding at the core... she tended to those inner shadows, those ugly parts in each of us that we pretend are not there, and searched relentlessly for truth... no matter what came up, she sat still in it... embraced it... affirmed it... she balanced her dance between weight and wander so well as she leaned deeper and deeper into the fullness of her being... her queerness... her complexity... her light... she allowed herself to change and evolve, to shed all that did not serve the womxn she was becoming... she refused to turn away from herself... she insisted so intently on healing...

brax reminds us that healing is never easy when you are a black womxn determined to be whole... that this work will be both sorrow and mourning... pleasure and play... peace and vitality... sadness and suffering... that embracing the duality of emotion is in fact the most essential part of the quest, because it invites us to accept the complexities of our own humanity... the blackness/ womxness/ queerness/ feminine/

masculine within us all... braxton's healing is an invitation into our own, a summoning for a collective quest into the blackgirl in each of us to reclaim all that was lost... to sit still with suffering and be silent in sorrow and face the feelings that feel unbearable... to find the purpose in our darkness... to ground ourselves unapologetically in our truth and to create from that place...

braxton remained so invested in learning to love her inner[blackgirl] child with all her heart... she let Little Brax guide her growth and lead her humbly into herself... she knew that even when she was alone with herself she was not by herself... that she was convening with God and her youth and the layers of herself, and all the ancestral spirits that gave her strength... and now she is with them, and now she is one of them... brax, baby child, truth teller, healer, we know you are healing in heaven, holding Little Brax close and letting her spirit fly free...

.

for hanu... my magical unicorn who grounds me in my britt britt, and for britt britt, who guides me to all things sacred... for all my friends who let me be my full whole self... for farima, lauren, marylin, angel, akilah, april, kerby, liza, lola, my aca support group, my flourish agenda family, my uc berkeley community... for all the friends i have loved and lost, for all the love i befriended and released... for sacred community that remains...

.

to my editor raina león, thank you from the bottom of my heart for the tenderness with which you received my work. thank you for affirming my love for black womxn, and for reflecting that love back to me. thank you to my publisher j. k. fowler and the entire nomadic press family believing in my poetry and for giving me the chance to tell this story. to micah bournes, thank you for being my very first editor, for telling me my work was dope when i could not believe it for myself. thank you to the editors of *fight evil with poetry* who published earlier versions of some poems featured in this manuscript.

reelaviolette botts-ward

is a homegirl, an artist, a writer, and an educator from Philadelphia, Pennsylvania. Founder of blackwomxnhealing (blackwomxnhealing. com), ree curates healing circles, exhibitions, courses, and research for and by Black womxn. As a doctoral candidate at the University of California, Berkeley, ree studies Black womxn's healing spaces in Oakland, using Black feminist poetics and artistry as tools for translation between academic and community audiences. ree received her BA from Spelman College and her MA from UCLA. Her work has been supported by UC Berkeley's Center for Race and Gender, Arts Research Center, Arcus Endowment, and the Alliance for the Arts in Research Universities, among others. She lives in Oakland with her beloved partner and two kittens.

OTHER WAYS TO SUPPORT NOMADIC PRESS' WRITERS

In 2020, two funds geared specifically toward supporting our writers were created: the **Nomadic Press Black Writers Fund** and the **Nomadic Press Emergency Fund**.

The former is a forever fund that puts money directly into the pockets of our Black writers. The latter provides up to $200 dignity-centered emergency grants to any of our writers in need.

Please consider supporting these funds. You can also more generally support Nomadic Press by donating to our general fund via nomadicpress. org/donate and by continuing to buy our books. As always, thank you for your support!

Scan here for more information and/or to donate.
You can also donate at nomadicpress.org/store.